Especially for

....

From

....

....

© 2011 by Barbour Publishing, Inc.

Compiled and written by Janice Hanna.

ISBN 978-1-61626-406-2

Published by Barbour Publishing, P.O. Box 719, Uhrichsville, OH 44683, www.barbourbooks.com

Our mission is to publish and distribute inspirational products offering exceptional value and biblical encouragement to the masses.

Member of the
Evangelical Christian
Publishers Association

Printed in China.

365 Creative Ways to

Beat
Stress

Stress-Free Inspiration for Every Day!

BARBOUR
PUBLISHING

Day 1

Change Your Perception

While situations, encounters, or events may seem intrinsically "stressful," it is truly how an individual perceives and reacts to an event that determines whether or not the stress response is activated.

CHARLES W. MAYO, M.D

Day 2

Work during
Your Creative Peak

Many of our stresses come
from "running behind" on our
work. Here's a key to improving
your work output: work during
your creative peak. Take your
temperature every two hours over
a twenty-four-hour period. Theory
is, you're most creative when
you're at your warmest.

Day 3

Look at the Stars

If the stresses of life have you
wound up tighter than a clock,
take a nighttime trip outdoors
to gaze at the stars. There's
nothing like stargazing to
remind you that Someone
far greater has everything—
large and small—under control.

Day 4

Color a Picture

Remember when you were
a kid. . .the hours you spent
coloring pictures? Maybe it's
time to try a little crayon
therapy again. Keep a coloring
book and crayons nearby.
When you're stressed,
pull them out and color—
inside or outside the lines.

Day 5

Guilt-Free Relaxation

The mark of a successful man
is one that has spent an entire
day on the bank of a river without
feeling guilty about it.

UNKNOWN

Day 6

Write in Your Journal

Writing is cathartic. It helps you "get out" those emotions. And there's nothing like "free-writing" (writing without lifting your pen) to say what's really on your mind. If you're truly stressed, pour it out on the page, not on the people you love.

Day 7

Staring

A poor life this if,
full of care,
we have no time
to stand and stare.

WILLIAM HENRY DAVIES

Day 8

Play with Children

Having a stressful day?
Why not revert to childhood?
Get down on the floor with the
kids, and play with building
blocks or other creative toys.
Once your imagination is
fully engaged—and you've
shared in a few chuckles with
the kids—your troubles
will be far behind you!

Day 9

Don't Worry. . .Be Happy

"Who of you by worrying can add a single hour to your life? Since you cannot do this very little thing, why do you worry about the rest?"

LUKE 12:25–26 NIV

Day 10

Get a Pet

Did you know that
pet owners are often less
stressed than non-pet owners?
There's something about
sitting with a dog or cat at
your side—stroking, cuddling,
relaxing—that forces you to let
go of the cares of the world.

Day 11

Do-Si-Do

Many of us remember a time
when school students had
to learn to square dance as
part of their physical education.
Next time you're stressed, put
on some music and do a little
do-si-do around the living room.
You'll de-stress and get some
exercise at the same time!

Day 12

More Than an Overcomer!

*"I have told you these things,
so that in me you may have peace.
In this world you will
have trouble. But take heart!
I have overcome the world."*

JOHN 16:33 NIV

Day 13

Watch What You Eat

Did you know that certain
foods act as triggers for pain
and sickness? Processed sugar,
for instance, can aggravate joint
pain, which can lead to stress.
If you're going through a tough
period, guard your diet. Your
stress level will decrease
as your body comes
into alignment.

Day 14

Move to a Different State

Stress comes from the state
of mind that what you're facing
is a life and death emergency.
Sometimes you just need to
move to another state (in your
mind/thoughts). Tell yourself,
"This too shall pass." What
seems like an emergency
today will be nothing but
a memory tomorrow.

Day 15

Keep a Stress Diary

If you're wondering what causes you to stress out, keep a stress diary. Whenever you're feeling stressed, write down the activities (or situations) you were experiencing at the time.

Day 16

Keep Things Tidy

Getting stressed out at home or in your office? Maybe it's time for a cleaning spree. Having a lot of clutter around can stress you out, whether you realize it or not. Put everything in its place so that you don't have to stress while searching for it later.

Day 17

Don't Tie Yourself to the Clock

Tick-tock, tick-tock. Oh, how we're tied to the clock. We live, eat, and breathe by it! Living by the clock can be a huge trigger for stress. As much as you're able, look away from the minute hand, and focus on the things (or people) at hand instead.

Day 18

Take a Walk

Sometimes we just need to
step away from our work, get out
of the house, and go for a walk.
There's nothing like a brisk walk to
relieve the stresses of the day.
And, if you're a dog owner,
take Rover along. Chances
are pretty good he could
use the walk, too!

Day 19

Start with the Smallest Problems First

Oy! How the problems can stack up. When we're facing a mountain of them, the stresses can be horrible. Your best solution? Tackle the problems one at a time, starting with the smallest and working your way up to the big stuff.

Day 20

Calgon, Take Me Away!

There must be quite a few things
that a hot bath won't cure,
but I don't know many of them.

SYLVIA PLATH

Day 21

Have a Plan

We live in a day and age when everything is planned out—our work schedule, our kids' sports practices, even our weekend activities. Why, then, don't we have a plan for stress? Put together a course of action for what you'll do the next time stress builds up.

Day 22

Be a Trash Disposal

If trash (stuff that leads to
stress) is piling up, take a day
and deal with it. Don't avoid it
any longer. Get rid of it. Let it go.
There! Doesn't that feel better?

Day 23

Get a Pedicure

Ah, the pedicure. Is there anything more glorious? There's something so relaxing about that bubbly, warm water and the intense foot massage. Relaxed feet lead to a relaxed body. So, pay the price. Go on! You can justify it. A clean foot makes for a happy, healthy mind.

Day 24

Peace, Peace, Wonderful Peace

"Peace I leave with you; my peace I give you. I do not give to you as the world gives. Do not let your hearts be troubled and do not be afraid."

John 14:27 NIV

Day 25

Breathe In, Breathe Out

The next time you're stressed out, try sixty seconds of slow, steady breathing. Slow things down a bit, and just b-r-e-a-t-h-e!

Day 26

Don't Be a People Pleaser

Much of our stress comes
from trying to make other people
happy. When we put God in His
rightful place, only His opinion
matters, not the opinions of
man. So, lay down your desire
to please people, and seek
only to please God.

Day 27

Take Up Painting

Tired? Stressed? Pick up a
paintbrush and fill your pallet
with magnificent color! Nothing
is more relaxing than painting.

Day 28

Call Worry Your Enemy

Sometimes we invite worry in
as a friend. We coddle it and
nurture it, as if it brings us
pleasure. We forget that
it's a leading cause of stress.
No more! It's time to call worry
your enemy! Don't accept it!
Be ready to battle it instead.

Day 29

Get Rid of Mind-Racing

Do you ever feel like thoughts are racing through your mind? Go, go, go! That's the pace between our ears. Today, take a deep breath. Slow those thoughts. You're not in a race. Give those hurried thoughts to the Lord, and watch as He envelops you with His peace.

Day 30

Watch Old TV Shows

Having a rough day?
Stressed out? Tune in to an old
television show, one you enjoyed
as a child. There's nothing like
an episode of "I Love Lucy" or
"Leave It to Beaver" to put
a smile on your face!

Day 31

Sleep In

Lack of sleep can lead to exhaustion, which can affect both your health and your attitude. Maybe it's time to sleep in. Take a morning off. Or catch a catnap in the afternoon. Go to bed an hour earlier. A little sleep goes a long, long way toward keeping you healthy.

Day 32

Join a Support Group

If you're stressed out but
can't seem to get things
under control, consider looking
for support groups in your area.
Specialized groups can
address needs that you might
be facing and will give you
others to communicate
with about your struggles.

Day 33

Identify Your Stressor

What's got you stressed out?
Lack of money? A heavy
workload? Half the time we
don't know what specifically
is causing the stress. It's time
to take inventory. Identify
your stressor, then deal
with it constructively.

Day 34

How Not to Find Peace

No one can get inner
peace by pouncing on it.

HARRY EMERSON FOSDICK

Day 35

Limit Your Pity Parties to Three Minutes

Everyone likes to throw a pity
party when she's stressed out.
Here's the key: Throw your party
but limit it to three minutes.
Set your timer and stress away!
But when you're done, you're done.

Day 36

Step Away from the Computer

Working hard on a project? Been staring at the computer screen all day? Maybe it's time to turn off the computer and step away. Even five or ten minutes away from the screen can be enough to lower your stress levels.

Day 37

Create a Recipe

There's nothing like cooking to de-stress you. And there's nothing more relaxing and enjoyable than coming up with your own recipe. You'll have the satisfaction of knowing you created it yourself, and you'll get to eat it afterward.

Day 38

Play Video Games as a Family

Playing games is always
a fun way to relieve stress,
but there's something so
enjoyable about family-themed
video games. Bowling, golf,
arcades. . .you can find
something for everyone
in the family.

Day 39

Don't Knee-Jerk

One of the leading causes
of stress in tough situations
is knee-jerking. We act impulsively
and live to regret it. Today,
make a point not to knee-jerk.

Day 40

Collect Coins

There's something so relaxing about the collection process, and what better thing to collect than rare coins? They hold considerable value and are a challenge to find. Why not start collecting today?

Day 41

Set Realistic Goals

One of the reasons we get
stressed out is because we take
on too much. We get in over our
heads and feel like we're drowning.
Today, begin to set realistic goals,
then work toward them,
inch by inch, day by day,
for a stress-free life.

Day 42

Relief in a Hurry

For fast-acting relief,
try slowing down.

LILY TOMLIN

Day 43

Listen to Music from Days Gone By

Remember those great songs from when you were young? If you're stressed out, maxed out, or worn out, why not browse the Internet until you find a copy of a song that made you feel great when you were a kid.

Day 44

Learn the Warning Signs

Imagine you're driving down
a highway and come upon a
warning sign: BRIDGE OUT AHEAD.
Would you keep driving?
Of course not. In the same
way, life gives us warning signs.
Stress is a sign that you're
overloaded. It's time to pay
attention to the signs.

Day 45

Chocolate

Mmm. . .chocolate!
There's nothing like a
nibble of dark chocolate on a
stressful afternoon to release
those endorphins. If you're feeling
stressed, keep a small supply
of dark chocolate nearby. Treat
it like you would an aspirin—
only one or two,
used sparingly.

Day 46

Find the Value in Doing Nothing

Don't underestimate the value of doing nothing, of just going along, listening to all the things you can't hear, and not bothering.

POOH'S LITTLE INSTRUCTION BOOK,

INSPIRED BY A. A. MILNE

Day 47

Understand Who's in Charge of Your Provision

Stressed out because you've got too much month and not enough money? The best way to overcome financial panic is to realize that you're not in charge of your finances. . .God is. When financial stresses come, hand them over to the One in charge.

Day 48

ASAP

The little letters ASAP
have come to mean "hurry, hurry,
hurry!" They increase our stress
level. The next time you see
them, however, let them
take on a new meaning:
"Always say a prayer."

Day 49

Pull Out the Knitting Needles

Knitting is a great way to overcome stress. While you're focused—knit one, purl one—you don't have time to get burdened down by life's woes. You're far too busy creating something of beauty.

Day 50

Stay Connected

We often let the stresses of life disconnect us from the people we love. If you're at the breaking point, don't withdraw. . .connect!

Day 51

Don't Lash Out

Lashing out is such a
temptation when we're stressed,
but it's not God's answer to
the problem. Today, as you
ponder the stresses in your life,
make a conscious decision
not to lash out.

Day 52

Be Prepared

One of the reasons we
get so stressed out is because
we're simply not prepared.
We want to cook a particular
meal, but we're missing
ingredients. We want to
paint a room but don't have
a paintbrush. Before you
begin a task, make sure you
have everything you need.

Day 53

Accentuate the Positive

Perhaps you remember the
old song about accentuating
the positive and eliminating
the negative. Never is it truer
than when you're stressed.
Look for the positive in your
situation. . .and you
will surely find it.

Day 54

Tense. . .and Release

This is a great technique for relaxing those muscles. Tense up for several seconds, then release. Do this several times in a row.

Day 55

Forget Your Troubles, C'mon Get Blogging

Like all forms of writing, blogging can be very therapeutic. What sets it apart from, say, writing in a private journal is the fact that your readers can respond to you, offering encouragement. Why not start a blog today?

Day 56

Massage

There's nothing more relaxing than a great massage. For one lovely hour, you can literally feel the tension leaving your body. A great massage affects body, mind, and spirit.

Day 57

Show Up Early

Always rushing to get
to events and appointments
on time? Perhaps that's adding
to your stress level. Take
inventory. . .and be honest.
Perhaps it's time to put
together a plan of action so
that you can arrive at your
appointments on time,
or even early.

Day 58

Keep Tabs on What You're Viewing (or Hearing)

Did you realize that the shows you watch on television and the songs you listen to on the radio can add fuel to the fire where your stress level is concerned? It might be time to change the station (or turn the television or radio off altogether).

Day 59

Fatigued Nerves

We live longer than our forefathers; but we suffer more from a thousand artificial anxieties and cares. They fatigued only the muscles, we exhaust the finer strength of the nerves.

EDWARD GEORGE BULWER-LYTTON

Day 60

Don't Make It a Lifestyle

There cannot be a
stressful crisis next week.
My schedule is already full.

HENRY KISSINGER

Day 61

RAK

The best way to get around
stress is to turn your attention
off yourself and onto someone
else. When you're really maxed
out emotionally, try performing
random acts of kindness.
Choose someone in your
circle of friends,
and bless them
unexpectedly.

Day 62

Keep Those Relationships in Balance

How often do we get caught up in unbalanced relationships? We let people drain us then wonder why we're stressed out and exhausted every time they come around. It might be time to take a little "friendship inventory" to make sure everything's in balance.

Day 63

Listen to Classical Music

Mozart, Beethoven, Schubert, Bach. . .there's nothing like the lyrical flow of classical music to steady your nerves. If your blood pressure's rising, reach for the Tchaikovsky and watch those stresses roll away, like fingers across the piano keys.

Day 64

Take Your Vitamins

Stresses high? Maybe your
vitamin levels are low. This might
be a good time to take stock
of your A, B12, and C.

Day 65

Don't Exaggerate

We're skilled at making things bigger than they really are, but doing so only adds stress to our already harried lives. If you'll downplay events instead of exaggerating them, you might just convince yourself that they're not such a big deal after all!

Day 66

Everything in Running Order

Broken faucets. Toilets
that don't work properly.
A toppled fence. There's nothing
like a house that's falling apart
to keep you stressed. Today,
take inventory of the things
in your home that need to be
repaired. . .then get to work!

Day 67

Learn to Play an Instrument

The rhythmic and methodical
movements associated with
playing an instrument are very
beneficial in the quest to get
rid of stress. Even if you've never
played an instrument in the
past, now's the time to learn.
Soon you will be able to
play your troubles away!

Day 68

Avoid Hot-Button Topics

Some of our stresses are self-induced. We raise hot-button topics just to get a rise out of someone, then find ourselves in a heated conversation. To avoid stress while in a group, stay away from trigger topics!

Day 69

Take Your Hands Off

How we love to be in charge.
We take the reins in our
hands and hold tightly to them.
We somehow think we can
fix everything. But we're not
in the fixing business.
Aren't you glad God is?

Day 70

Take flight

Give your stress wings
and let it fly away.

TERRI GUILLEMETS

Day 71

Visit Your Local Coffee Shop

Sometimes just getting
away from your environment
is enough to calm you down,
and what better place than your
local coffee shop. Whether
you're a coffee aficionado or
not, the aroma will be soothing
and the ambience calming.

Day 72

Send Your Dog to Obedience School

Dogs are known as man's best friend, but sometimes they're a huge source of stress, too! They chew your shoes, gnaw the leg of the table, spread toilet paper around the house. To rid yourself of stress, take Fido to obedience school. It will be good for both of you!

Day 73

Lower Your Pressure Levels

Live always, my friend, as if there is world enough and time.

MEYER FRIEDMAN

Day 74

Learn to Laugh at Yourself

One of the reasons we get so stressed out when things don't go the way we planned is because we don't know how to laugh at ourselves. Learning how to let go and laugh—really truly laugh—will take us a long, long way in the battle against stress.

Day 75

Go Back to School

If you're really inundated
with stress, you might consider
taking a class in a subject helpful
to your situation—conflict
resolution, for instance.
The classroom environment
just might be the thing
to get you over the hurdle.

Day 76

Ignore Your Critics

Why, oh why do we care so much what other people think about it? If you're inundated with criticism, remember. . .only the Lord's opinion matters!

Day 77

Spend Time in God's Presence

Want to know the ultimate stress reliever? Spend time with the Lord. Crawl up into His lap. Let Him convince you that the things you're stressing over are only temporary problems, not eternal issues.

Day 78

Call a Friend

Truly stressed?
Can't take it anymore?
Maybe you just need a listening
ear. Pick up the phone and call
someone who loves you.

Day 79

Build Model Airplanes

This might seem like an
odd way to deal with stress,
but building things—especially
on a model scale—can be
relaxing. As you focus on
those small parts, fitting them
together to take flight—imagine
your problems being "fitted
together" by the Lord so
that you have wings to fly.

Day 80

Deliver Meals on Wheels

Next time you're feeling stressed,
why not sign up to help others
less fortunate? Deliver meals
on wheels and spend a little
time getting to know
those on the receiving end.

Day 81

Appreciation

Each day brings both joys
and sorrows. For some reason,
it's easier to focus on the
sorrows (trials, problems,
sadnesses) than the joys.
Today, spend some time
appreciating the good
things your day brings!

Day 82

Organize

"A place for everything,
and everything in its place."
Perhaps you've heard the old
adage. It's more important in the
twenty-first century than ever
before, because we have so much
stuff. . .and stuff leads to stress!
Find a place for that stuff,
and keep it there.

Day 83

Our Response

Stress is not what happens
to us. It's our response to
what happens. And response
is something we can choose.

MAUREEN KILLORAN

Day 84

Release the Reins

Oh, how we hate to admit
that we're not in control of
our lives. Thinking that we hold
the reins adds all sorts of
pressure we don't need,
spiritually, emotionally,
and physically. Today, if you've
been trying to hold tight
to the reins of your life,
release them to God.

Day 85

Finish Something

We're great at starting
things, but sometimes finishing
them seems impossible.
However, there's nothing
more satisfying than finishing
something you've started.
If you're stressed out,
think of something
you can finish.

Day 86

Feeling Warm
and Fuzzy All Over

Ah, the sauna. It opens
the pores, loosens the
muscles, warms our bodies,
and gives us a "secret place"
to meet with the Lord!

Day 87

Stop Procrastinating

"I'll do it tomorrow."
How many times have you
said those words? If you're
looking to lower your
stress levels, stop
procrastinating
and get to it!

Day 88

Consider a New Hairdo

Here's a unique tip
for relieving stress:
consider a new hairdo.
Sometimes when
we're feeling down
— or stressed—
a makeover can make
all the difference!

Day 89

Bake Bread

Don't you love the aroma of bread baking? There's nothing like it. It conjures up images of childhood and soothes the soul. Next time you're stressed out, try baking a loaf of bread.

Day 90

Laughter

Laughter is a gift from God,
sure to cure the blues and lift
your focus when you're stressed.
There's something about
that "bubbling up" in your
belly that makes all the
bad things go away.

Day 91

Teapot Theology

Releasing the pressure,
it's good for the teapot and
the water. Try it sometime.

JEB DICKERSON

Day 92

Wear a "Stress Less" Button

Here's a fun idea.
Make a button that reads
"Stress Less!" Wear it on
days when you're liable to be
stressed. If you can't wear it,
then attach it to your
laptop bag, your purse,
or your briefcase.

Day 93

Get a Hand Massage

When our bodies get tense,
our hands are often the worst.
Visit your manicurist for a
luxurious hand massage.
Feel the tension leaving
through those fingertips.

Day 94

Drive

There's nothing better than
a long drive on a country road
to make you forget about your
troubles. Get behind the
wheel and drive, drive, drive.

Day 95

No One's Perfect

Believing that you must
do something perfectly is a
recipe for stress, and you'll
associate that stress with
the task and thus condition
yourself to avoid it.

STEVE PAVLINA

Day 96

Pull Out the Treadmill

Many of us own a treadmill but don't use it. When you're stressed, consider walking away your troubles. Rain, snow, sleet, or hail. . .it doesn't matter when you're treadmill-bound!

Day 97

Dance in the Rain

Remember that old Gene Kelly movie *Singin' in the Rain*? There's no better way to overcome stress than to have a "praising your way through the storm" attitude. Today, instead of stressing over your problems, lift up your voice in song and start tapping those toes!

Day 98

Take Your Work Outdoors

We spend so much of our
day indoors. Often work dictates
that we must. Consider taking
your work outdoors. Sit at
a patio table to type, to send
e-mails, to make calls.
Just being out of your
ordinary environment
will lift the spirits.

Day 99

Cut Back on Caffeine

Nothing is worse for the nerves than caffeine. We think we have to have it to wake us up but end up addicted. Today, make a decision to slowly wean yourself from caffeine.

Day 100

Attitude, Attitude, Attitude

Adopting the right attitude
can convert a negative stress
into a positive one.

HANS SELYE

Day 101

Sponsor a Child

There are many wonderful
stories in the Bible
about generosity. If you're
stressed about finances (or
anything else, for that matter),
consider sponsoring a child in a
third-world country. You will be
giving out of your need,
and it will put your
financial woes
in perspective.

Day 102

Cardio

A quick cardio workout will distract you from your problems, will get your heart working, will burn calories, and will serve as a great stress reliever!

Day 103

The Most Important Thing

Sometimes the most
important thing in a whole day
is the rest we take between
two deep breaths.

ETTY HILLESUM

Day 104

Embroidery

Straight stitch, cross stitch, knotted stitch. . .pull. There's something so relaxing about watching a vibrantly colored thread ease its way along a white piece of fabric. And the end result? A beautiful work of art you can use in your home!

Day 105

Automatic Payments

Ever been stressed out because you forgot to pay a bill? Maybe the lights were shut off or the water trickled down to a drip? Consider setting up automatic payments on your monthly bills so that you can rest easy month-to-month.

Day 106

Enjoy Nature's Bounty

Climb the mountains and
get their good tidings.
Nature's peace will flow into
you as sunshine flows into
trees. The winds will blow
their freshness into you, and
the storms their energy,
while cares will drop off
like falling leaves.

JOHN MUIR

Day 107

Hot Tub

The hot tub. . .oh, what
a wonderful idea! No matter
what kind of day you've had,
you can climb into that
bubbly hot water, lean back,
and let the jets work their
magic on your weary muscles!

Day 108

Give Your Talents to God

Today, spend some time in prayer.
Ask the Lord to show you the
gifts, talents, and abilities He
has given you. Then release them
into His hands so that He
can use you as He will.

Day 109

Plant a Garden

When the world wearies
and society fails to satisfy,
there is always the garden.

MINNIE AUMONIER

Day 110

Get in the Habit

We have so many habits, don't we? Some are great (reading our Bible every day, praying, etc). Some aren't so great (gossiping, procrastinating, and so on). The not-so-great ones can serve to raise our stress levels. Today, make up your mind to create a new, healthy habit!

Day 111

Kid Stuff

Stressed out? Overworked?
Need a break? Pull out a funny
kid's video. Dance with Dora.
Dream with the Backyardigans.
Travel with Diego. Let yourself
think like a kid again!

Day 112

The Rubber Ball Method

Sometimes our stress pulls us down, and we think we can't get back up again. Today, make up your mind to bounce back. Think of the rubber ball. It hits the floor, then shoots straight back up again, often higher than before!

Day 113

Candle-Making

So, you've been burning
the candle at both ends?
Feel like you're almost
burned-out? Why not try
something like candle-making
to help you relax? The physical
act of making a candle will forever
remind you that God never
intended the candle to
burn from both ends.

Day 114

Urgent!

I try to avoid stress—it makes
me feel like I'm rubber-stamping
all my organs URGENT.

BERRI CLOVE

Day 115

The Ultimate Smiley Face

Remember that little yellow smiley face we used to see? Find a picture of one, and keep it nearby at all times—near your workstation, on your computer screen, on a bumper sticker. Sometimes we just need that little reminder to smile.

Day 116

Pay Tribute

If you're battling adversity,
struggling through a situation
that has you stressed out, think
of a person in your family who has
overcome great challenges. Send
a little note of encouragement,
and thank that persistent
loved one for sticking with
it. Doing so will help you
stick with it, too!

Day 117

Aromatherapy

Mmm, those lovely smells! Did you know that scents can greatly affect our mood? If you doubt it, try spending a little time in a room filled with fertilizer! Surround yourself with lovely aromas to remain calm, cool, and collected.

Day 118

Spend Time with
God Every Day

We rush from here to there,
trying to meet with friends,
loved ones, coworkers, bosses,
and neighbors. Sometimes,
in the quest to meet with so
many, we forget to meet with the
One who longs to see us most.
Today, make up your mind to
spend time with God daily.

Day 119

Sample a Delicacy

Here's an exciting way to overcome stress! Try a little gourmet chocolate. Or maybe a nibble of an expensive cheese. Nibble some caviar, or try a truffle or escargot. "Treating" yourself to a delicacy will surely help you in the battle against stress.

Day 120

Bird-Watching

He's sitting outside your window,
just waiting. . .wondering if you'll
sneak a peek! He's a blue jay,
a cardinal, a wren, a sparrow,
a finch. There he sits, on the tree
limb, wondering if you'll grab your
binoculars, lay down your work,
and pay him a little attention.

Day 121

Mosaics

Consider the mosaic.
Tiny bits of broken glass or
pottery are repieced, forming
something beautiful out of
something that was once broken.
As you work to create a
beautiful piece, see your own
life in Christ—once broken,
now a thing of beauty.

Day 122

Live in the Moment

We mourn over yesterday,
fret over tomorrow, and
sometimes forget to live in
the day we've been given. Grab
ahold of today and live
it for all it's worth!

Day 123

Celebrate!

There's nothing like a
great party to lift your spirits.
If you're feeling down, why
not throw your own personal
party? The guest of honor? God!
Celebrate the magnificent
things He has done for you.

Day 124

Invest in an E-Reader

Reading is so relaxing, but not when you've run out of books. If you find yourself trekking back and forth to the library, consider investing in an e-reader, instead. You'll find hundreds of free books on the web, available to download with the click of a button!

Day 125

Join a Prayer Group

Praying is the best thing
we can do when we're stressed.
But the Bible is clear that
corporate prayer (where two
or more are gathered) is
especially powerful. If you're
feeling stressed, consider
joining a small group, where
you'll be surrounded
by people who will
pray for you.

Day 126

Go to the Library

Your local library is a peaceful place—quiet, calm, relaxing. It's filled with great books to take your mind off your troubles, and librarians ready to help you find the books you need. If you're stressed out, consider a trip to this special place.

Day 127

Learn to Delegate

Have you ever said the words, "Oh, just give it to me and let me do it!" Sometimes we take on tasks that were never meant for us, simply because we think we can do it best. It's time to let go. Delegate! Give those tasks away!

Day 128

Grab Your Fishing Pole

There's something so relaxing
about the fishing experience.
Perhaps that's one reason
we find so many fishing stories
in the Bible. So, what's keeping
you? Grab your rod and reel
and head for the lake!

Day 129

Squeeze It!

If you're all wound up and looking for a way to "un"-wind, try investing in a squeezable stress reliever. It will work the muscles in your hand, which will calm and soothe your troubled mind.

Day 130

Memorize the Serenity Prayer

God grant me the serenity to accept the things I cannot change; courage to change the things I can; and wisdom to know the difference.

REINHOLD NIEBUHR

Day 131

A Healthy Sex Life

We try everything we can to relieve stress but often overlook one of the greatest gifts God ever gave to us. For married couples, an enjoyable sex life helps us maintain a strong relationship and relieve the day's stresses as well.

Day 132

Buy a Bicycle

Remember that joyous
feeling you had as a kid when
you climbed up on your bicycle and
rode with the wind in your hair?
How freeing! How stress relieving!
So, what's stopping you now?
Maybe it's time to purchase
a bike and hit the trails!

Day 133

Sit Up Straight!

Remember how your mother used to correct your posture when you were young? Turns out, she was right. Our posture is especially vulnerable when we're sitting at the computer. To avoid hand and arm strain, sit up straight!

Day 134

Balance Ball

Stress can start in the
neck and work its way down the
back. Purchase and use a balance
ball to keep those vertebrae
loose and happy!

Day 135

Snap Some Photos

Ah, photography! Don't
you love to take pictures—
of nature, buildings, people,
and so on? There's something
so relaxing about seeing
life through the eye
of the camera.

Day 136

News Break

The stresses we face in
our personal life are enough,
but add to that national and
global traumas, and you've
got a recipe for disaster.
To ease your mind and lower
your stress, take a break from
the news for a few days.
You might miss a few stories,
sure, but your stress
level will be lower.

Day 137

Cry

Tears are a wonderful gift from God. They offer a sense of physical and emotional release. Many people don't like to cry because they think it makes them weak. Just the opposite! Use that God-given gift of crying as it was intended, and watch your stresses fly away.

Day 138

Delete!

What a crazy day and
age we live in! Our e-mail
boxes overflow—with letters,
work-related things, and junk.
Sometimes we live and die by
what we find in our inbox. It's time
for that to change, especially
if you're feeling overwhelmed.
Don't let your inbox take over
your life, and don't be afraid
to hit the delete button.

Day 139

A Trip Down Memory Lane

Looking for something to
take your mind off things?
Help you chill out? Pull out
those old photographs
and take a trip down
memory lane.

Day 140

Loosen Up!

Clothes can be a pain. . .literally!
We wear jeans that are too tight,
or shoes that pinch our toes.
Whether we recognize it or not,
this can stress us out. It's
time to loosen up! Wear
comfortable clothes and
shoes, and your mind and
thoughts will respond.

Day 141

Sketch It

Sketching is a great way to
relieve stress. Grab your tablet
and pencil, and sketch to your
heart's delight!

Day 142

Look for Miracles Every Day

There's an old saying: "If you look for miracles, you will surely find them." Today, spend some time in search of a miracle. When you find it, all the difficult things you're facing will suddenly be seen in perspective.

Day 143

Single-Task

We twenty-first-century
worker bees are great at
multi-tasking. We take on
several projects at once and pay
a heavy price. To alleviate stress
in your life, stop calling yourself
a multi-tasker, and begin
to single-task once more.

Day 144

Pull from Your Resources

Over your life you've
accumulated so much—stuff,
skills, experiences, and so forth.
When you're stressed out or
facing a problem that seems
too big, try reaching into the
goody bag of things you've
already learned from
prior experiences.

Day 145

Let's Talk about It

How many stresses are caused from poor communication? We say something and it's misconstrued, or maybe we misunderstand something someone else has said. It's time to hone our communication skills. Why not start today? Make a point to avoid misunderstandings.

Day 146

Cast Your Cares

If you've ever been fishing,
then you know what it means
to "cast" your line. That's exactly
what God wants us to do when
we're beaten down by life's cares. . .
cast them on Him. Start
today by letting go of what
troubles you. Envision casting
it into His capable hands.

Day 147

Avoid Difficult People

Oy! Difficult people! They seem to confront us at every turn. Some are unavoidable; others are not. If you've got difficult people in your life, do what you can to keep your distance. Don't let their drama roll off onto you.

Day 148

Memorize the Word

There's nothing like scripture
to keep you focused. When you
quote the Word of God, you see
yourself as an overcomer.
One of the best ways to memorize
scripture is to place your
favorite verses around
your house—on mirrors,
the refrigerator,
your doorpost, etc.

Day 149

S-t-r-e-t-c-h

Tension comes from muscles
being tightly knotted. To alleviate
the pain, stop every hour on
the hour and stretch your neck,
your shoulders, your arms,
and your fingers.

Day 150

Have an Attitude of Gratitude

Remember when you were
a kid and someone would shout
"Attitude check!" You would
respond with "Praise the Lord!"?
Today, allow the Lord to give
you an attitude check.
May you be found with an
attitude of gratitude!

Day 151

Break Out of Your Rut

Do you ever feel like you're
stuck in a rut? Can't get
out? Today, ask the Lord to
springboard you out of your rut.
As you face new experiences,
new places, new faces,
the pressures of the
rut will be released.

Day 152

Can I Catch a Ride?

If you're one of those people who gets stressed out because you have to drive to work alone, it might be time to find someone you can commute with. You can split the costs and develop your friendship.

Day 153

Volunteer

Most of us who are overloaded assume we don't have time to volunteer, but it's time to reconsider. There's something so rewarding about giving of your time—at a hospital, a homeless shelter, a ministry at your church. Talk about taking your eyes off your own problems!

Day 154

See Each New Day as a Gift

Remember that feeling of excitement you got as a child when you would unwrap your birthday presents? Today is a gift. It's just as exciting as any present you've ever received. When we see each day as a gift, we focus more on the blessing and less on the problems.

Day 155

Accept Your Personality

Maybe you're a choleric, take-charge kind of person. Perhaps you're melancholy or phlegmatic. You need a little extra push to keep going. Maybe you're a bubbly sanguine, always ready to party, but not to work. Knowing and accepting your personality will help you know how to handle life's stresses!

Day 156

Bathe in Epsom Salts

There are many benefits
to taking a warm bath. It melts
away life's struggles for a few
glorious minutes. Adding Epsom
salts to the water is an excellent
way to invigorate those
weary muscles and prepare
you for the tasks ahead.

Day 157

Saturday Morning Cartoons

Remember sitting in front
of the television on Saturday
morning, still dressed in your
jammies, a bowl of cereal in
your hand? What a blast!
It's still a great way to
decompress after a
long, stressful week.

Day 158

Become a Helper

One of the reasons we get
so stressed out is because we
want to be the boss. We like to
be in charge. Today, ask the Lord
how you can play second fiddle.
Become a helper—to a friend,
a coworker, or a family member.

Day 159

Watch Reruns of Comedy Shows

Most of us grew up watching entertainment (or variety) shows. They were filled with wacky skits, fun song and dance numbers, and even some stand-up comedy. Today, spend some time browsing the web to locate a DVD of your favorite childhood comedian or comedienne.

Day 160

Get to the "Root"
of the Problem

If you're stressed out,
headachy, or tired, here's a quick
tip: visit your local hair salon for
a shampoo and scalp massage.
Having someone else wash your
hair for you can be very relaxing,
and the massage will work to
ease your troubles as well.

Day 161

Never Call
Yourself a Failure

I have not failed. I've
just found ten thousand
ways that won't work.

THOMAS ALVA EDISON

Day 162

Collect Sea Shells

Have you ever walked along the seashore, marveling over the ocean? Have you reached down to pick up an exquisite seashell? Truly the majesty of the simple shell—shaped and formed in that mighty ocean—is enough to convince you that God can be trusted to shape us as well.

Day 163

Do Nothing

There's never enough time to
do all the nothing you want.

BILL WATTERSON, *CALVIN AND HOBBES*

Day 164

Girls/Guys Night Out

When we get stressed out,
we tend to spend time alone.
Getting with your girlfriends
(or guy friends) is a great
way to forget your troubles
and just get happy.

Day 165

Retreat to Eden

To sit with a dog on a hillside
on a glorious afternoon is to be
back in Eden, where doing nothing
was not boring—it was peace.

MILAN KUNDERA

Day 166

Color Me Lively!

Remember how you used
to use crayons and markers
to pass the time when you were
young? It's never too late to
pull them out and get creative.
The art of putting color on
a white page can be very
stimulating, and gives you
the perfect outlet to get
rid of your stresses.

Day 167

Don't Borrow Trouble

God never intended for us
to carry our own troubles, let
alone those of our friends and
family members. If you're weighted
down with care, take inventory.
Is it possibly you're trying to
fix something for someone
else? If so, the time has
come to let it go.

Day 168

Avoid the 911 Mentality

Stress is an ignorant state.
It believes that everything
is an emergency.

NATALIE GOLDBERG

Day 169

Stop the Critiques

Do you have an internal editor?
Is he/she always critiquing—you,
those around you, those in
your family? If so, shut down
that editor. Critique almost
always leads to stress.

Day 170

Don't Lean on Your Own Understanding

Trust in the LORD with all your heart and lean not on your own understanding.

PROVERBS 3:5 NIV

Day 171

Here Ducky, Ducky!

If you're having a rough day,
head to your nearest park.
Go straight to the lake or pond,
and feed the ducks. You'll be doing
them a service and getting rid of
stresses at the same time.

Day 172

Put Together a Puzzle

There's something rather
wonderful about putting together
a puzzle, isn't there? As you fit
together those pieces, stresses
flee. And the picture you're
creating is a great reminder
of the life you're now living,
which the Lord is piecing
together, day by day.

Day 173

Travel the World (by Internet)

Always wanted to travel? Limited by time or resources? No problem. Put together a make-believe trip, using places you find on the Internet. Travel from country to country (site to site), and experience the culture, the music, and the architecture. By the end of the journey, you will find that your stresses have disappeared.

Day 174

Take Advantage of the One Life You Have

I shall pass through this
life but once. Any good therefore
that I can do, or any kindness
I can show, let me do it now.
Let me not defer or neglect
it. For I shall never pass
this way again.

ETIENNE DE GRELLET

Day 175

Don't Create
Unnecessary Drama

If you're like most people,
you sometimes make mountains
out of molehills. You over-react.
Take this vow today: "I'll keep
my drama on the stage where it
belongs." No unnecessary
over-reacting. No blowing things
out of proportion. Even-keeled
responses will rid you of
your stress and create
a calm environment.

Day 176

Use Your Imagination

Some of the secret
joys of living are not found by
rushing from point A to point B,
but by inventing some imaginary
letters along the way.

DOUGLAS PAGELS

Day 177

Woodworking

Are you one of those people who enjoys working with his or her hands? If so, you would probably enjoy woodworking. Whittle away your troubles as you work and shape that piece of wood into something beautiful.

Day 178

Memorize a
Cheerleading Chant

Remember those great cheers
from high school football games!
"Ra-ra-shish-boom-bah!" When
the everyday pressures build,
just chant them away!

Day 179

Do the Right Thing

Always do right.
This will gratify some people
and astonish the rest.

MARK TWAIN

Day 180

Paint by Numbers

Don't you wish life was as easy
as one of those paint-by-number
pictures you worked on as a kid?
As a reminder that God knows
which color goes in which
space of your life, why
not purchase a
paint-by-number
picture today?

Day 181

Turn Everything Off

Oh, the noises that blare
around us! They can be
deafening at times, bringing
confusion and chaos. If you're
feeling discombobulated,
turn everything off. Turn off
the television, the radio,
the computer, the phone.
Everything. Turn it off,
and spend some time
in absolute silence
before the Lord.

Day 182

Employ Generosity

Blessed are those who
can give without remembering and
take without forgetting.

ELIZABETH BIBESCO

Day 183

Become a Nature Lover

God's beautiful creation surrounds us—rocky mountains, sandy shores, green trees, flowering plants, grassy fields. Whenever you're feeling stressed, pause a moment and drink in from nature's bounty. Experience the beauty of God's holiness through His creation.

Day 184

Shop for Bargains

Shopping isn't always the best way to beat stress, particularly if you're low on money. However, bargain shopping—particularly if you're purchasing things you really need and can truly afford—can be a great way to de-stress.

Day 185

Back it Up!

Here's a fun way to distract yourself from a stressful situation: count backward from 100! By the time you get into the eighties, you will be so distracted that you won't remember to be anxious!

Day 186

Give Yourself a
Wrestling Name

Here's a wacky idea to keep you
from getting stressed out. Give
yourself a wrestling name. Might
just come in handy when you're
battling the enemy of your soul.

Day 187

Ah, Rest!

Rest is not idleness,
and to lie sometimes on the
grass under trees on a summer's
day, listening to the murmur of
the water, or watching the clouds
float across the sky, is by no
means a waste of time.

J. LUBBOCK

Day 188

Set Up a Home Spa

Don't you love spa days? There's something about being pampered to make you forget your troubles. If you're unable to afford a day at a spa, then turn your home into one! Invite a friend or loved one over and swap massages, pedicures, etc. What fun you will have!

Day 189

Restore an Old
Piece of Furniture

There's something so
uplifting about restoring
furniture, isn't there? Stripping
it down to the bare bones,
then watching it spring back
to life again. Restoration is a
therapeutic process, one
that might just help
you through a
stressful time.

Day 190

Follow Your Secret Passion

Is there something you've always longed to do but haven't? Some childhood dream, perhaps, that has been shelved. Following your passion is a great way to de-stress and to see the future as a hopeful place.

Day 191

Sleep Deprivation

Let's face it. Between work, family, holidays, and so on, we're worn-out—physically, emotionally, and spiritually. To avoid added stresses during the Christmas season, commit to getting a full night's sleep every night.

Day 192

Steady. . .Steady!

We human beings are so fickle—
we feel strongly about something
one day and forget about it the
next. If you're going through
major stresses, perhaps it's
a wake-up call. Are you having
your daily time with the Lord?
Reading the Bible? Praying?
These are all areas where
steadiness really pays off!

Day 193

Go On a Picnic

Feeling overworked? Tired?
Grab a blanket, a picnic basket,
and a friend, then head to the
nearest lake or park for an
old-fashioned picnic!

Day 194

Roller Skate

Remember what it was
like when you were young?
You could skate for hours,
never growing tired. There was
something so freeing about
sailing around and around that
rink. Well, what's holding you back?
To alleviate your stresses, strap
on the skates and get to rolling!

Day 195

Tea for Two

One of the greatest things
you can do when you're maxed
out is to visit your local tearoom
or café. There you will be treated
like royalty and will nibble on
some of the yummiest treats
ever. Next time you're feeling
stressed, head out for
a tea party!

Day 196

Understand the Seasons

Live each season as it passes;
breathe the air, drink the
drink, taste the fruit, and
resign yourself to the
influences of each.

HENRY DAVID THOREAU

Day 197

Date Night

Overwhelmed with the kids?
Housework getting to you?
Trouble on the job? No problem.
Grab the one you love, and head
out for a date night. . .just the
two of you! It will make you
feel young again and give
you a break from life's
everyday stresses.

Day 198

Give Yourself a Travel Destination

If you could go anywhere in
the world, where would you go?
Paris? Vienna? Rome? Why not
plan a trip to that location?
Even if you can't go now,
you'll have everything in
place when the time comes.

Day 199

Write a Book Review

We often turn to books
for comfort, then close them
and walk away when we're done.
Why not write a book review online?
That way, you'll always remember
how good the book made you
feel, and you'll be doing the
author a favor, too!

Day 200

Use Hammer and Nails

Swinging a hammer is a
great stress reliever, believe it
or not. And striking a nail with a
hammer is an art form!

Day 201

The Eyes of a Child

Remember how much you
loved summer as a child?
Those carefree days at the pool.
Hanging out with friends. Eating
hot dogs and ice cream cones.
Maybe it's time to see
summer through the eyes
of a child once again.
Talk about a great
stress reliever.

Day 202

Rock Tumbling

If you've ever collected or tumbled rocks, you know the satisfaction of taking something dirty and jagged and polishing it into a thing of beauty. Not only does this process relax us, it's a reminder that the Lord is smoothing out our rough spots and polishing us into His image.

Day 203

Put Up a Bird Feeder

Putting up a bird feeder is
always a lovely idea—for both
you and the birds! It's one way to
bring nature to your doorstep. As
you watch those birds feeding,
may it remind you that the God
of the universe feeds and clothes
you. He is your provider!

Day 204

Check In, Check Out

If you're battling stress,
consider checking into a hotel
for a night. The change of
location will make you feel
like you're on a holiday.

Day 205

White-Water Rafting

If you've ever been rafting, then you know that you have to learn to work with both the current and the waves. It's the same with the things that cause you stress. Today, focus on working with your circumstances, not against them. Keep that boat afloat!

Day 206

Walk Barefoot in Rain Puddles

Remember that awesome feeling you had as a child as you splashed in rain puddles? Well, what's stopping you? As you kick that water up with your feet, you'll be kicking away your troubles.

Day 207

Plant a Tree

Perhaps you've planted trees to represent various milestones in your life—the birth of a child, for instance. Today, give thought to planting a tree as a reminder that your roots run deep in the Lord. Place it outside your favorite window to offer comfort on rough days.

Day 208

Skip instead of Walk

When you were young,
skipping just came naturally
to you. Why walk when you could
skip? That little skip in your step
represented a carefree spirit.
It's time to be carefree again!
Give your troubles to the Lord
then skip your way toward
a healthy life.

Day 209

Shred Your Worries

Worries can pile up,
no doubt about it. Here's
a great exercise to help when
you're overloaded. Write down
your worries—every one—then
shred them in your shredder.
This physical demonstration
can be a practical reminder
that we need to let go. . .
and let God.

Day 210

Visit an Aquarium

Watching fish swim in
an aquarium can be very
therapeutic, very relaxing.
We get caught up in their
beautiful colors, the way they
easily move through the water.
The next time you're feeling
stressed, head to
the aquarium.

Day 211

Go Swimming

Swimming is great exercise, but it's also great for the mind and spirit. There's something so wonderful about moving through the water, feeling that weightlessness. It's a lovely reminder that God stands by, ready to carry our burdens for us.

Day 212

Row, Row, Row Your Boat

Remember that wonderful childhood song about rowing your boat gently down the stream? What a lovely metaphor for facing problems as an adult. See yourself in that boat, rowing, rowing, rowing down a gentle stream. Tensions have to go as you give way to the gentle flow.

Day 213

Try New Foods

Have you ever given thought to the idea that you eat the same foods day in and day out? Maybe it's time to try something completely different. If you don't want to try new foods, then switch up your meals—have breakfast for dinner, or vice versa.

Day 214

1 + 1 = Too Much
to Think About

Oh, that to-do list. How it
controls us! Here's a great piece
of advice to keep you from getting
stressed out: don't add to your
to-do list until you've taken things
off. Otherwise, things will pile up!

Day 215

Pay a Little Visit

When you're tempted to turn your focus inward to yourself, just say these words, "Pay a little visit." You can visit a neighbor, a relative, or a friend on the computer, but take the time to "pay a little visit" when you feel stress coming on.

Day 216

COPE

When you've reached the
end of your rope, it's truly time
to COPE: cancel out problems
effectively. There's only one way
to do that—you've got to give
them away. To truly cope
means to kneel at the feet
of Jesus and pass your
problems to Him.

Day 217

Be an Encouragement to Others

How are you known among your peers? Do they see you as a positive, upbeat person? Or are you known as someone who's always stressed out? Starting today, make up your mind to be known as an encourager. Spend your days—even the stressful ones— offering uplifting words.

Day 218

Take a Mental Vacation

We can't always take a real
vacation, but there's always time
for a mental one. Close your eyes.
What do you see? The canals of
Venice? The pyramids? The Eiffel
Tower? Visit those places in your
imagination, and when you return,
your stresses will be gone.

Day 219

Take Deep Breaths,
Every Hour on the Hour

If you're facing a long
day—one filled with anxious
moments—try deep breathing
exercises every hour on the hour.
Slowly breathe in and out, doing
all you can to still your body
and relax your mind. There!
Doesn't that feel good?

Day 220

Jump Rope

You might not be able to jump rope like you did as a child, but you can envision yourself jumping over those problems that cause you stress. Start swinging the rope. It's time to jump!

Day 221

Float on the Water

Oh, the feeling of floating carefree on the water. If you've had a rough day, hit the water. Flip over onto your back and let your body float atop the water. You can literally feel the pressures of the day floating on up to the heavens.

Day 222

Don't Give Way
to the Spirit of Fear

When you're burdened,
it can be tempting to give in to
fear. Don't do it! Instead, take
inventory. How many times are
the words "Fear not!" used in the
Bible? Research each instance,
then apply the "Fear not!"
technique to your own life.

Day 223

Place a Tea Bag on Your Eyes

This is such a lovely idea!
If you like to break for tea at
some point during the day,
use moistened tea bags on your
eyelids. They will help get rid of
puffiness and dark circles and
will help you feel refreshed.

Day 224

A Shortage

If people concentrated on
the really important things in life,
there'd be a shortage
of fishing poles.

DOUG LARSON

Day 225

Visit a Chiropractor

Many of our stresses originate
in our neck, shoulders, and back.
If you're struggling with ongoing
physical stresses in these
areas, give thought to visiting
a chiropractor, who can
help you bring everything
into alignment.

Day 226

Decorate a Room
Any Way You Like

Changing the décor in a home
can be a great way to rid yourself
of stress. Paint the walls any
color you like. Add artwork and
décor, then furnish the space in
a way that will make you smile.
There's nothing like a spiffy
new space to lift the spirits.

Day 227

Shoot the Lone Ranger

If you're a lone ranger type (someone who insists on doing everything without help) here's a thought. . .perhaps it's time to kill off the lone ranger. Put an end to the "me, myself, and I" mentality. We were never meant to go through life alone, after all. We need each other!

Day 228

Shine Like a Diamond

The only difference between a diamond and a lump of coal is that the diamond had a little more pressure put on it.

ANONYMOUS

Day 229

Build a Sand Castle

Remember the joy
of building a sand castle
when you were a youngster?
The creative process was
invigorating, and the final
product always made you
feel so good about what
you had accomplished. If
you can't get to the beach,
then head out to your
child's sandbox. . .
and get busy!

Day 230

Visit an Art Gallery

Exquisite works of art can both inspire and relax us. There's something rather awe-inspiring about artwork that was created hundreds of years ago. It has stood the test of time, and serves as a reminder that we, too, can stand the test of time. . .with God's help.

Day 231

Remember Something That Made You Laugh

Whenever you're feeling burdened down, think back to the last time you laughed. . .really, truly laughed. What motivated that laughter? A story? A child's antic? A coworker's joke? Revisit that place, and let the giggles begin!

Day 232

Be Affectionate

Even if you're not affectionate
by nature, there's something so
special about cuddling—with a
child, a grandchild, a spouse,
a pet, or a stuffed animal—to
make you forget your troubles.
Try a little cuddling today!

Day 233

Mow the Lawn

Need to work through some stress? Grab the lawn mower and get busy mowing your yard! As you push your way through those stubborn obstacles (blades of grass), see yourself pushing through life's troubles with just as much ease.

Day 234

Go to the Arboretum

Oh, the flowers! They're alive
with color, lining the walkways of
your local arboretum in brilliant
display. And they're just what the
doctor ordered on a stressful day.
Stop to smell the roses. . .
at your local garden
or arboretum.

Day 235

Throw Cold Water on It

When a wildfire hits, the only solution is water. Sometimes the same thing is true of the challenges we face. When things heat up—internally, with a friend, between you and a family member—think like a firefighter. Throw water on it, and watch the flames disappear.

Day 236

Do It Anyway

I am always doing that which
I cannot do, in order that I
may learn how to do it.

PABLO PICASSO

Day 237

Lengthen Your Fuse

Sometimes we're our own worst enemies. We get wound up so tight because our fuse is too short. The Bible instructs us to be patient, so it's time to lengthen your fuse. As you do, you'll give yourself time to react properly.

Day 238

Be a Team Player

Sometimes we add stress
to our already heavy workload
because we don't play well with
others. We bully them or refuse
to work alongside them. It's time
to lay down that nonsense and
become a team player. You'll
feel better. . .and so will
the rest of the team!

Day 239

Locate a Stress Chair

If anxiety is an ongoing problem for you, then pick out a certain chair in your office or home that you label your "stress chair." Whenever you feel anxiety coming on, head to the chair, to separate yourself from your troubles.

Day 240

Eat Something Crunchy

It's a proven fact that crunchy snacks can help relieve stress. Instead of reaching for potato chips, though, you might try carrot sticks, celery, or rice cakes. You'll get the same results, but with far fewer calories.

Day 241

Build Your Own Library

If you're an avid reader—
particularly to overcome life's
stresses—why not take the
time to build your own library?
Start with proper bookshelves,
then separate the books
according to genre. Alphabetize
them by author's name. That
way you'll never have to
go searching for a book.

Day 242

White Noise

The hum of a fan,
the gurgling sound of
a water feature, instrumental
music. . .all these things provide
what is known as "white noise,"
noise that doesn't interfere
with your daily work.
If you're feeling a little
stressed, turn on the noise!

Day 243

Strength Undefeatable

Life is either a daring
adventure or nothing. To keep
our faces toward change and
behave like free spirits in
the presence of fate is
strength undefeatable.

HELEN KELLER

Day 244

Have a "Remember When" Party

If the stresses of the grown-up world are too much, invite friends your age and older to a "remember when" party. You can play games you played as kids, dress in the garb from "your day," and swap stories about the good old days.

Day 245

Our Father Who Art in Heaven

So many times we offer
up popcorn prayers—shooting
them hard and fast at the ceiling.
If you face a morning drive to the
office, why not spend that time in
concentrated prayer?
The time will pass quickly,
and your prayer life
will grow exponentially.

Day 246

Take Up Bowling or Golf

There's nothing like your favorite sport to calm you down when the going gets rough. If you can't join a bowling league or hit the golf course, try the video versions of these games. They're almost as much fun, and just as relaxing!

Day 247

Tres Bien?

Learning a second language can be a great way to step outside your own (sometimes trying) situation. Doing so will also open doors for you to communicate with a whole new group of friends. Who knows what God will do!

Day 248

Reframe Your Situation

Imagine the situation you're now facing as a picture in a frame. Maybe it needs a new frame. How you "frame" (see) your situation is critical. Have you framed it as something that will be your undoing? If so, reframe it and call yourself an overcomer!

Day 249

A Happy Disposition

Smiling through the pain
doesn't come naturally. And
keeping a happy disposition when
you're stressed doesn't either.
But both are possible,
and both will energize you
to keep on keepin' on.

Day 250

The Eternal Optimist

We don't always feel like optimists, especially when we're hard hit by situations. Even if you haven't been a "glass is half full" sort of person, make up your mind to be. Start calling yourself an optimist, even if you don't feel like it.

Day 251

Design Your Own Castle

Feeling like you're going
nowhere in life? Has your
situation got you feeling
stressed? Blue? Here's a fun
antidote. Design a castle—
everything from the moat to the
tower. You'll have a lot of fun,
and will be left with a feeling
that you can conquer
kingdoms after-the-fact.

Day 252

Big Shot

A big shot is a little
shot that kept shooting.

ANONYMOUS

Day 253

Upbeat or Downbeat?

What sort of people do you surround yourself with? Positive and upbeat or critical and downbeat? Perhaps you're feeling beaten down because of the company you keep. Time to do inventory! Spend more time around positive people, and they will rub off on you.

Day 254

Remember You're Not Alone

So do not fear, for I am with you; do not be dismayed, for I am your God. I will strengthen you and help you; I will uphold you with my righteous right hand.

ISAIAH 41:10 NIV

Day 255

Close Your Eyes

Imagine you're in the
middle of a stressful situation.
You're not sure what to do.
There's no escape. . .or is there?
Why not try closing your eyes for
ten to twenty seconds. Doing
so will physically separate you
from the problem and give you a
moment to think more clearly.

Day 256

Are You Listening?

Oftentimes our prayers
are ushered heavenward one
after the other. We don't take
time to pause and listen for
God's response. If you're going
through a "heavy" season,
it's especially important to
get God's perspective.
Don't just talk. . .listen.

Day 257

Rearrange the Furniture

Overwhelmed? Stressed?
Thinking you'll never break
out of the rut you're in? Why
not rearrange the furniture?
Giving a room a makeover
will make everything around
you feel fresh and new.

Day 258

Purchase Pretty Teacups

Many of us who get stressed
out turn to hot tea, but don't
pay attention to how it's served.
Instead of that ugly mug you
usually use, treat yourself to
an exquisite tea set. That way,
when you're really stressed,
you'll have something lovely
to look at while you sip.

Day 259

Cling to the Rock

He only is my Rock and my Salvation; He is my Defense and my Fortress, I shall not be moved.

PSALM 62:6 AMP

Day 260

Unclench

If your teeth are clenched and
your fists are clenched, your
lifespan is probably clenched.

TERRI GUILLEMETS

Day 261

One Muscle at a Time

When your body has reached
its limit and your muscles are
tied up in knots, try progressive
muscle relaxation. Lie on the
floor. Start with your feet.
Stretch and release. Work
your way up, consciously
relaxing very muscle
along the way.

Day 262

Do the Work

Have you been stressing over
a task that seems too big?
Weighted down before you even
begin? Here's a great idea: do the
work. Just do it. Get in there,
dig your heels in, and get the
job done. The task won't kill you.
Likely, it will make you stronger!

Day 263

Swap Stuff

Sounds crazy at first glance,
doesn't it? But swapping stuff
can give you—or your home—
a whole new feel. Whether it's
clothes, furniture, drapes,
or wall decor, swapping with
a friend can be great fun,
and a great stress reliever.

Day 264

Get Caught

*Slow down and everything
you are chasing will come
around and catch you.*

JOHN DE PAOLA

Day 265

In Sickness and in Health

If you're battling illness, take
the time to heal before diving
back into the work. You do
more harm than good when
you plow through. In fact,
if you're not careful, you'll
elongate the illness.

Day 266

Celebrate What
Jesus Did for You

Life's problems pale in the
light of what Jesus did for us on
the cross. If you're overwhelmed,
pause from what's ailing you,
and take the time to celebrate
what was done for you over two
thousand years ago. His sacrifice
will put our woes in perspective.

Day 267

Choose Your Thoughts

*The greatest weapon
against stress is our ability to
choose one thought over another.*

WILLIAM JAMES

Day 268

The Will to Win

Do you have the will to win this
battle against stress and anxiety?
If you're not ready to win, then
you're not ready for the battle.

Day 269

Ooo, Lights!

A fun way to change your mood is to change the lighting. Spend a little time trying different colored bulbs—in your office, your bedroom, your bathroom, etc. All the areas where you spend time should be comfortably lit to create the calmest possible environment.

Day 270

The Little Things

When you hear the words
"emotional investment" what
comes to mind? We invest ourselves
in a great many things, don't we?
Some are large and require our full
attention. Others are small and do
not. Today, make a point not
to invest yourself in the little,
inconsequential things.

Day 271

Enjoy a Sunset

Oh, the colors of a brilliant sunset!
The reds, golds, oranges, and so on
can captivate us, taking our breath
away. Funny. . .when we're standing
breathless before a gorgeous sunset,
we forget all about our troubles.
Perhaps God intended it that way.

Day 272

The Golden Rule for Coworkers

Stress among coworkers
can get out of hand at times.
Today, make up your mind to apply
the Golden Rule to those you
work with. Treat them just
as you would want to be
treated. . .and watch
the stresses fly!

Day 273

Sing Your High School Song

Facing a troubling situation?
Wish you could find a way out?
Try singing your high school song.
It's a fun way to lift your spirits,
and a great memory-booster!

Day 274

Nutrition

Good nutrition is vitally important, especially when we spend our days working, working, working. If you're not feeling up to par—if you're more stressed than usual—then take a close look at your diet. Perhaps you're not getting all the nutrients you need.

Day 275

Can We Talk?

Some call it chitchat. Others call it "hanging out with friends." Some call it conversation. Regardless of what you call it, take time to engage with other people today. Doing so will shift your focus and remind you that you are not alone.

Day 276

Blow Bubbles

Remember those little bottles
of bubbles you used to play with?
They're just as effective now as ever!
To make your own, put a few drops
of dish detergent in water. . .
and have at it! Fill the yard
with bubbles and watch your
troubles pop, pop, pop!

Day 277

Give a Hug

There's something so comforting about a hug, especially when you're troubled or feeling weighted down. Whether you're on the giving or receiving end, a hug always makes everything better. Make it a point to hug someone today.

Day 278

Wacky Café

Here's a creative way to rid
yourself of stress. Stop what you're
doing and put together a menu for
a make-believe restaurant. Give the
meals funny names. For that matter,
give the restaurant a funny name.
By the time you're done,
all your stresses will be gone.

Day 279

Follow Your Bliss

Perhaps you've heard the
expression "Follow your bliss."
Following after the thing you love
helps keep you focused, especially
on the tough days. The Bible teaches
us to put the Lord above everything
else. In other words, He is
our bliss. We must follow
wholeheartedly after Him.

Day 280

Your Best Interest

Who has your best interest
at heart, some might ask. Most
of us would answer, "I do!" There is
only One who truly has your best
interest at heart. He knows your
yesterdays, your todays, and
your tomorrows, and you can
trust Him every step
of the way.

Day 281

Don't Forget to Live

Sometimes we forget that
work is not the important thing.
Living is. Sure, we have to work.
We have to pay bills. Things get
hard. But beyond all that, we must
take time to really, truly live.

Day 282

Take a Break

A life spent in constant labor
is a life wasted, save a man be such
a fool as to regard a fulsome
obituary notice as ample reward.

GEORGE JEAN NATHAN

Day 283

Simplify

Can you imagine what life would be like without all our modern "necessities"? Perhaps it's time to find out. Spend a day giving up several of the things you count on—Internet, television, cell phone, etc. You may find that simplifying will rid you of extra burdens.

Day 284

Use Your Artistic Gifts

Do you act? Sing? Dance?
Are you a painter, a storyteller,
a poet? All these artistic gifts
were given to you by the Lord.
He longs for you to stir them
up and use them for Him.
What a great way to say
good-bye to stress!

Day 285

Dream On!

Part of the reason we get
so weighed down by life is that
we've lost our ability to dream.
Remember all those plans you
had as a teen? Remember being a
starry-eyed twentysomething?
Perhaps it's time to breathe
life into some of those
dreams again.

Day 286

Ignore the Bully

Don't let your mind bully your
body into believing it must carry
the burden of its worries.

ASTRID ALAUDA

Day 287

Dear Friend. . .

When you're overanxious or
feeling blue, it's always good to reach
out to a friend. Perhaps you have a
good friend—someone who meant
the world to you—who's moved away.
This is the perfect day to write a
wonderful, heartfelt letter.

Day 288

Join in the Dance

Toddlers are so carefree.
They don't know enough about
life to be burdened down by worry.
When you turn on their favorite
television show, they dance
around the room, arms
extended. What about you?
Maybe today is the day
to join in the dance!

Day 289

Take a Cooking Class

Have you ever been to cooking school? If you're interested in the art of cooking, this is the perfect creative outlet. It's also a great way to rid yourself of tensions. You'll have something to look forward to, and something great to eat as well!

Day 290

Can I. . .or Can't I?

One key ingredient to releasing stresses is to figure out what you can control. . .and what you can't. Once you know what's not yours to control, you won't waste unnecessary time trying. You can focus on the things that really are yours to deal with.

Day 291

Tell a Tall Tale

Today, spend some time telling your child (or niece or nephew) a story about a grandparent or great-grandparent they never knew.

Day 292

An Aromatic Reminder

To remind yourself to stay calm
in tough situations, try dabbing
a bit of essential oil—peppermint,
eucalyptus, hyssop, juniper,
or another soothing scent—
on your wrist. You'll have a
yummy-smelling reminder
not to panic!

Day 293

One Bite at a Time

Facing a huge problem? Don't know how you're going to get through it? Take it one small bite-size piece at a time, tackling only what you can handle in the moment. Before long, all the bites will be eaten and you'll still be stress-free.

Day 294

Skip Rocks into a Lake

How long has it been since you've stood at the edge of a lake or pond with stones in your hand? Wouldn't it feel good to send those stones sailing across the water, just like you did when you were a kid?

Day 295

Exercise

Sit-ups, toe-touches,
shoulder rolls. . .ah, how good
they are for you. And what great
stress relievers. If you're really
tight (especially in the neck
and shoulders), put on your
workout gear and dive in!

Day 296

Flush Your Stress with Water

Did you know that dehydration can cause all sorts of problems, physical and otherwise? Most people don't get enough water. Next time you're feeling stressed, reach for a big, tall glass of water.

Day 297

Seek Solitude

Remember the story of Jesus
in the Garden of Gethsemane?
He went away from the disciples
for a time because He needed time
to pray. If you're stressed. . .
seek solitude. Escape from
the maddening crowd—
even your circle of
friends—and pray.

Day 298

One, Please!

Whenever you're feeling
burdened, think in ones: one day
at a time, one thing at a time.

Day 299

Rushed No More

Stuck in rush-hour traffic?
Facing a long drive home from the
office? This is a great time to listen
to sermons or other motivational
speeches you've downloaded onto your
MP3 player. You won't get as worked
up about the traffic, and you will be
blessed by what you hear.

Day 300

A Fun Post

If you're looking to lift your
spirits and alleviate stress, try
leaving fun messages (or posts) on
a friend's blog or social media page.
Make your friend's day by saying
something flattering or by leaving
an encouraging scripture.

Day 301

Take Up Scrapbooking

Oh, the joy of scrapbooking.
It's everything rolled into one:
a creativity booster, a trip down
memory lane, a way to deal with
all those photographs. It's also
an awesome way to relieve
anxieties. Why not start
a scrapbook today?

Day 302

*Do not be anxious about anything,
but in every situation, by prayer
and petition, with thanksgiving,
present your requests to God.*

PHILIPPIANS 4:6 NIV

Day 303

Decide Not to Decide

Sometimes the rush to make
a decision adds extra pressure
we don't need. There are some
situations where we can simply decide
not to decide. . .at least not in the
moment. When you're under a
tremendous amount of stress,
decide not to decide.

Day 304

Redefine Urgency

Is everything as urgent as
your stress would imply?

CARRIE LATET

Day 305

Eliminate Debt

Being in debt can be so stressful.
As you enter this, the month
where we celebrate Thanksgiving,
begin to seek the Lord for how you
can get out of debt so that you
will have one more thing to
be thankful for!

Day 306

Sing Silly Songs

There's nothing like a goofy song
to lift your spirits when you're
weighted down with life's cares.
The next time you feel like wringing
your hands, sing a happy
tune instead.

Day 307

Keep That Neck Warm!

Stress is carried in the muscles around the neck. One great way to alleviate the tension is to use a neck warmer. If you don't own one, you can easily make one using cotton fabric, white rice, and the essential oil of your choice to give it the best possible aroma.

Day 308

Figure Out What's Important

So many times we have our priorities out of whack. We think we know what's important but really don't. So we get stressed out over things that really are of little consequence. It's time to reanalyze. Figure out what's really important. Then ask the Lord to help you keep everything prioritized.

Day 309

Improve On the Worst

First ask yourself: What is
the worst that can happen? Then
prepare to accept it. Then proceed
to improve on the worst.

DALE CARNEGIE

Day 310

Get Off the Fast Track

Zoom, zoom, zoom! We fly from
here to there, work to home, church to
social events, then wonder why we're
exhausted and stressed. Today, make
a conscious decision to slow down.
Get off the fast track,
and your nerves—and body—
will thank you.

Day 311

Volunteer at a Homeless Shelter

November is the best time
of year to think about volunteering
at a homeless shelter. Sure, this is
a busy season for you. Likely you're
overwhelmed. But think about those
less fortunate. Give them a reason to
give thanks this season by
serving them with a smile.

Day 312

Unwind

Do you ever wish the clock
would move backward? That you
could go back—unwind—and remove
some of the pressures that have
stacked up? Today, ask the Lord
to do a spiritual "unwinding,"
so that you can face today—
and tomorrow—stress free.

Day 313

Praise the Lord

Oh, what a wonderful way to overcome life's challenges! We're taught in the Word of God that praising the Lord in the very midst of the battle is the way we win. If you're facing an enemy of any sort today—stress, heavy workload, family troubles— praise the Lord!

Day 314

Release Your Pain

Perhaps you're one of the millions around the globe who struggles with chronic pain. It wears you out, and wears you down. The pressure to keep going in spite of the pain is intense. Today, make a conscious effort to release that pain into the hands of the only One who can bear it.

Day 315

Write a Short Story

Writing is a cathartic process.
With every word that hits the page,
you're releasing a bit of yourself.
If you're battling through a difficult
season. . .write. Pen stories, articles,
or books. Get it all down on the
page, and watch the Lord work
through your own words.

Day 316

Thrive!

Those who've been through
a lot of personal tragedies have
a "just make it through" mentality.
Instead of seeing yourself as a
victim, make a list of all of the
tragedies you have survived.
Then make up your mind to
not just be a survivor. . .
but a thriver!

Day 317

Nurture Kindness

If you've ever raised a child,
you know what it means to
nurture. Some people nurture
their pain, giving it a higher place
than they should. Today, make
a point to nurture kindness,
even if you're walking through
a difficult season. Offering
kindness heals others. . .
and yourself.

Day 318

Don't Focus on Success

It's one thing to want to succeed;
it's another to succeed at any cost.
When our health begins to fail, when
our sleep patterns are interrupted,
it's time to redefine success. What do
you really want, anyway—God's idea
of success, or your own?

Day 319

Cut Back on Sugar

Getting all hyped up on
sugar might be fun in the moment,
but there's a terrible letdown on
the other side of it that can cause
depression, fatigue, and stress.
If you're particularly low, then
give some thought to cutting
back on the sweet stuff. It's
not so sweet in the end!

Day 320

Get a Reality Check

Reality is the leading cause of stress
for those in touch with it.

JANE WAGNER

Day 321

Spend a Day in Your Jammies

Oh, the luxury of a day in your pajamas. Is there anything more calming?

Day 322

Build Strong Friendships

Friends—true friends—stick with us in good times and bad. That's why it's especially important to build such strong friendships, so you don't have to walk through life's valleys alone. Today, make up your mind to build strong and lasting friendships that will weather every storm.

Day 323

Become a Stargazer

There is precious little hope to
be gotten out of whatever keeps us
industrious, but there is a chance
for us whenever we cease work
and become stargazers.

H. M. TOMLINSON

Day 324

Be an Actor

If you find that you're
frequently getting worked up,
ask yourself a question: "Am I an
actor or a reactor?" Be honest!
Reactors carry things too far,
making too big a deal out of things.
Today, make up your mind not to
react in the flesh but rather to
act—according to the Word.

Day 325

Your Estimation

If you are distressed by anything external, the pain is not due to the thing itself, but to your estimate of it; and this you have the power to revoke at any moment.

MARCUS AURELIUS

Day 326

A Neighborly Gift

When we're loaded up with stress, when we're overworking ourselves, we sometimes miss out on what's in front of us. Today, pay particular attention to the people around you. Is there someone— a lonely neighbor, perhaps—that you can bless with a small gift?

Day 327

Talk to God about
What Stresses You Out

Remember that old song, "Have
a Little Talk with Jesus"? There's
never a better time than when you're
stressed out. Instead of running
to friends, sugar, or television,
start with the Lord. He's
right there. . .waiting.

Day 328

Memorize Three Clean Jokes

There's nothing like a great joke to lift you out of your humdrumness. "Hey, did you hear the one about. . . ?" "A pastor, a priest, and a rabbi get on a boat. . ." Memorize three clean jokes, then pull them out when life's stresses build.

Day 329

A Positive Ending

Everything is okay in the end.
If it's not okay, then it's not the end.

UNKNOWN

Day 330

Put Your Hope in the Lord

*But those who hope in the L*ORD *will renew their strength. They will soar on wings like eagles; they will run and not grow weary, they will walk and not be faint.*
ISAIAH 40:31 NIV

Day 331

Praise-Fest!

It's hard to focus on your own woes when you're busy praising others. Think of someone you're exceptionally proud of and spend some time giving praise where praise is due. You'll be surprised at how it lifts your spirits, too!

Day 332

Why Worry?

It makes no sense to worry
about things you have no control
over because there's nothing you
can do about them, and why worry
about things you do control?
The activity of worrying
keeps you immobilized.

JOELY FISHER

Day 333

Guard Your Self-Talk

Sometimes we stress ourselves out with our self-talk. We sabotage ourselves by saying things like, "I can't handle this," "This is too much," or "I'll never make it through this." Change what you say, and watch your stress levels drop.

Day 334

Apply Humility

We're taught in the Bible to humble ourselves in the sight of the Lord. Though it's hard to do, it's great for our health. For, when we puff ourselves up, we put far too much emphasis on our own strength, our own performance. Humility goes a long, long way in reducing the tension!

Day 335

Sabbath Rest

Take rest; a field that has
rested gives a bountiful crop.

OVID

Day 336

Seek Lasting Peace in God

We search everywhere for peace—
the workplace, relationships,
hobbies—and instead find turmoil.
As you approach this Christmas
season, lay aside your desire to
find answers in earthly things.
Seek lasting peace—the kind
that will change your life
forever—in the God
who created you.

Day 337

Stress Is. . .

Stress is the trash of modern life—we all generate it, but if you don't dispose of it properly, it will pile up and overtake your life.

DANZAE PACE

Day 338

Known. . .and Loved

Sometimes we can feel so
alone during the holidays. Our
emotions get tied up in a knot.
We don't feel like celebrating
because of feelings of aloneness
or betrayal. This Christmas, take
heart! The God who made you
knows you. . .and loves you!
You are never truly alone.

Day 339

Lie Down in Green Pastures

The LORD is my shepherd,
I lack nothing. He makes me lie
down in green pastures, he leads
me beside quiet waters,
he refreshes my soul.

PSALM 23:1–3 NIV

Day 340

Engage. . .Don't Withdraw

Oh, how we're tempted to
withdraw when we're anxious or
frustrated, especially during the
holidays. Who feels like getting
in the holiday spirit when they're
facing real problems, after all?
But God desires that you spend
this Christmas season fully
engaged—with His children,
and with Him.

Day 341

Spend Time in the Holy of Holies

Looking for a great getaway? Look no further than the holy of holies—that secret hiding place where you can spend time at the Lord's feet, sharing your burdens and being re-energized for the tasks ahead.

Day 342

Half our life is spent trying to
find something to do with the
time we have rushed through
life trying to save.

WILL ROGERS

Day 343

Ho-Ho-Holidays

Trying to get in the holiday spirit
but struggling through personal
stresses? Try making your
own Christmas cards. As you
write those jolly well-wishes,
your spirits will be lifted!

Day 344

Kill Off the Nag

Do you ever hear that little
voice inside, nagging, nagging,
nagging. . .telling you that your
life will always be like this? That
things will never get better?
Today, make a conscious
decision to kill off the nag!

Day 345

Beading

There's a wondrous joy in creating things of beauty. Lovely necklaces, pretty bracelets, dangly earrings—these are all things you can make with colorful beads. Beading shifts your focus away from your troubles. Best of all, you can give away the jewelry as a Christmas gift!

Day 346

Visit a Nursing Home

If the stresses of life are weighing on you, then grab your kids, your neighbors, your friends from church, and visit a local nursing home. Take along home-baked goodies. Sing Christmas carols. Put on a little Christmas play. You'll find that your spirits are lifted as you give the gift of Christmas cheer.

Day 347

Build a Gingerbread House

Oh, what fun! Christmas just wouldn't be Christmas without gingerbread houses. Too old to build one, you say? Never! It's very therapeutic, after all! As you construct that colorful house, spend time thanking God for the many ways He has been at work in your life, building you into a mighty man or woman of God.

Day 348

Baking for Others

If you're feeling overwhelmed, then baking is a great stress reliever. Instead of baking for yourself, however, give some thought to baking cookies or sweets for relatives, neighbors, or loved ones. They'll love the presents. . .and you'll love the process!

Day 349

Give Those Burdens to Jesus

"Come to me, all who are weary and burdened, and I will give you rest. Take my yoke upon you and learn from me, for I am gentle and humble in heart, and you will find rest for your souls. For my yoke is easy and my burden is light."

MATTHEW 11:28–30 NIV

Day 350

Mr. Postman, Look and See. . .

Here's a fun idea to get your eyes off your own troubles: leave a gift in your mailbox for the mailman. What a great way to turn your focus to someone else during the holidays.

Day 351

Wear Funny Socks or Underwear

Are you facing a more-than-usually stressful day? If so, do yourself a favor and wear funny socks or underwear. No one will see them, but you'll know they're there. Then, when the turmoil begins, you can laugh your way through it, thinking about what's hiding underneath.

Day 352

Indulge in Little Luxuries

Sometimes it's nice to
treat yourself—to a spa day,
an afternoon off, a massage,
an ice cream cone. Anything to
divert your attention away from
your troubles. What sort
of luxuries are you
craving today?

Day 353

Be in the Now

Yesterday's the past, tomorrow's
the future, but today is a gift.
That's why it's called the present.

BIL KEANE

Day 354

Take a Time-out

Remember what it was like
to give your child a time-out?
He had to sit in the corner with
his nose to the wall. Well, it's
time for a grown-up time-out!
Turn your face away from
your troubles to a quiet,
peaceful place.

Day 355

Once Upon a Time

The holidays can be so crazy,
can't they? If you're feeling the
pressure, then pause a moment,
and think of a special Christmas
story you can share with your
children or grandchildren. Maybe
you could share a tale about your
very best Christmas ever.

Day 356

Give the Gift of Gift-Wrapping

Here's a creative way to
get your eyes off your own
troubles—offer to wrap
Christmas presents for
someone who can't.

Day 357

Sing "Rudolph the Red-Nosed Reindeer"

Feeling blue? Lost in the chaos of Christmas shopping? Tired of standing in long lines at the checkout? Next time you're in a stressful Christmas situation, just begin to sing "Rudolph the Red-Nosed Reindeer." Before long, your troubles will fly away!

Day 358

Go to the Toy Box

Think of your favorite childhood
toy. Was it a car? A train? A doll?
A wood-burning kit? Likely you got
hours of pleasure out of that toy.
Why not surf the Internet until
you find that toy? Purchase
it, and play until your
stresses are behind you.

Day 359

Remember the
Reason for the Season

Christmas can be a stressful time
of year. We rush here and there,
buying, wrapping, cooking, cleaning.
Today, on this special holy day,
pause to remember the reason
for the season. Without Him,
nothing else matters.

Day 360

Recommit Your
Life to the Lord

What has this past year
looked like for you? Was it filled
with stresses and concerns?
Troubles aplenty? Why not
recommit yourself to the Lord
as you face this new year?
Commit to walk with Him,
hand in hand, no matter
what life brings your way.

Day 361

Don't Over-Schedule or Over-Commit

It's so hard not to over-commit yourself, isn't it? It's easy to look at the calendar and see all the things you should (or could) be doing. But over-commitment and over-scheduling will always lead to over-stressing. So, remove the "overs" from your vocabulary today.

Day 362

Create a Daily Schedule

As you look ahead to the next year, spend some time working on a daily schedule. If you lay out a practical plan of action, setting realistic goals for yourself— day by day, hour by hour—then you'll lessen the risk of becoming exhausted or stressed out.

Day 363

Visit Your Doctor for a Check-up

If you've spent much of the past year in a stress-out state, this would be a great time to schedule an appointment with your doctor to make sure you're in tip-top shape.

Day 364

Remember Life Runs in Seasons

Winter, spring, summer, and fall. . .the Lord God (truly) made them all. And He longs for you to enjoy each one, including the transitions in between. If you're feeling stressed or fatigued, remember, "This too shall pass." So, hang on! Seasons are (always) about to change!

Day 365

A Fresh Start

Don't you love do-overs?
They're such a blessing. As you
close out one year and head into
another, praise the Lord for a new
year and a new start. May
your next year be your
most stress-free ever!

Notes ....
....
....
....
....
....
....
....
....
....
....
....

Notes.....................................

....

....

....

....

....

....

....

....

....

....

Notes..
....
....
....
....
....
....
....
....
....
....

Notes..
....
....
....
....
....
....
....
....
....
....
....

Notes

Notes ....

....

....

....

....

....

....

....

....

....

....

Notes ....
....
....
....
....
....
....
....
....
....
....
....

....

....

....

....

....

....

....

....

....

....

....